GREAT FILMMAKERS
PETER JACKSON

Wil Mara

Cavendish
Square

New York

Published in 2015 by Cavendish Square Publishing, LLC
243 5th Avenue, Suite 136, New York, NY 10016

Copyright © 2015 by Cavendish Square Publishing, LLC

First Edition

No part of this publication may be reproduced, stored in a retrieval system, or transmitted in any
form or by any means—electronic, mechanical, photocopying, recording, or otherwise—without
the prior permission of the copyright owner. Request for permission should be addressed to
Permissions, Cavendish Square Publishing, 243 5th Avenue, Suite 136, New York, NY 10016. Tel
(877) 980-4450; fax (877) 980-4454.

Website: cavendishsq.com

This publication represents the opinions and views of the author based on his or her personal
experience, knowledge, and research. The information in this book serves as a general guide
only. The author and publisher have used their best efforts in preparing this book and disclaim
liability rising directly or indirectly from the use and application of this book.

CPSIA Compliance Information: Batch #WS14CSQ

All websites were available and accurate when this book was sent to press.
Library of Congress Cataloging-in-Publication Data

Mara, Wil.
  Peter Jackson / Wil Mara.
    pages cm. — (Great filmmakers)
  Includes filmography.
  Includes bibliographical references and index.
  ISBN 978-1-62712-942-8 (hardcover) ISBN 978-1-62712-944-2 (ebook)
  1. Jackson, Peter, 1961- —Juvenile literature. 2. Motion picture producers and directors—New
Zealand—Biography—Juvenile literature. 3. Screenwriters—New Zealand—Biography—
Juvenile literature. I. Title.

PN1998.3.J26M38 2014
791.4302'3092—dc23
[B]

                                            2014003271

Editorial Director: Dean Miller   Senior Designer: Amy Greenan
Editor: Fletcher Doyle   Production Manager: Jennifer Ryder-Talbot
Senior Copy Editor: Wendy A. Reynolds   Production Editor: David McNamara
Art Director: Jeffrey Talbot   Photo Researcher: J8 Media

The photographs in this book are used by permission and through the courtesy of: Cover,
1, Matt Sayles/Invision/AP; Paul Kennedy/Lonely Planet Images/Getty Images, 5; Richard E.
Aaron/Redferns/Getty Images, 8; pagadesign/E+/Getty Images, 9, 26, 42, 46, 57, 62, 66; www.
demilked.com/free-paper-textures-backgrounds, 9, 26–27, 42–43, 46–47, 57, 62, 66; Sergio
Schnitzler/Shutterstock.com, 10; Silver Screen Collection/Moviepix/Getty Images, 12; Michael
Ochs Archives/Moviepix/Getty Images, 16; Mike Theiss/National Geographic/Getty Images, 17;
Giulio Marcocchi/Getty Images, 19; KPA/Heritage Image/age footstock, 21; © Photos 12/Alamy,
25; Robert Patterson/Getty Images, 27; MIRAMAX/Album/Newscom, 29; © AF archive/Alamy,
31; Robert Patterson/Getty Images, 33; Joe Seer/Shutterstock.com, 35; Pool/Getty Images, 36;
© Photos 12/Alamy, 39; New Line/Wirelmage/Getty Images, 41; ChameleonsEye/Shutterstock.
com, 43; KATHY HUTCHINS Photography/Newscom, 45; Frederick M. Brown/Getty Images, 47;
© AF archive/Alamy, 49; Hulton Archive/Moviepix/Getty Images, 50; © AF archive/Alamy, 53; ©
Photos 12/Alamy, 55; Troy Wegman/Shutterstock.com, 59; Kevin Winter/Getty Images, 61; Hagen
Hopkins/Getty Images, 62; Hagen Hopkins/Getty Images, 66; Rex Features via AP Images, 67.

Printed in the United States of America

TN
B
JAC

GREAT FILMMAKERS
PETER JACKSON

1 A MOST WONDERFUL CHILDHOOD

A House at the Edge of the Sea

Peter Robert Jackson was born October 31, 1961 in a hospital in Wellington, the capital city of New Zealand. His parents were Bill, a wages clerk, and Joan, who had worked in a hosiery factory before Peter was born. Bill and Joan had both been born in England and moved to New Zealand in the early 1950s to escape the lingering hardships of the Second World War, which had ravaged most of Europe.

The New Zealand government, looking to lure citizens from abroad, promised fresh starts and new opportunities for many in their position, including free passage to the island, employment prospects, and housing possibilities. Bill and Joan met in 1951 while attending a rugby match, and they were married in November 1953. The couple purchased their first home shortly thereafter, a cottage along

Pukerua Bay on the North Island of New Zealand provided an excellent environment for the young Peter Jackson.

the rising shores of Pukerua Bay. Although it was small in size, the location was beautiful and the community close and supportive—perfect, in other words, to raise a family.

Joan Jackson was not able to have a child for an unusually long time, and at first the Jacksons were afraid that she might not be able to do so at all. Then, finally, Peter came along in 1961. Due to the difficulties of having a child so late in life (she was well into her forties by the time she gave birth to Peter), Joan would not have another baby.

Peter was given great attention and adoration as an only child, and yet by all accounts he did not become spoiled or selfish. Relatives on both sides of his family had followed Bill and Joan to New Zealand and settled close by, so he was often with his cousins, aunts, and uncles, as well as his many friends and neighbors in the close-knit Pukerua Bay area. Since Pukerua was regarded as safe and secure, Jackson and his companions were free to roam about and enjoy themselves.

Peter was also encouraged to let his imagination run wild. He was extremely creative, and such an idyllic setting provided the perfect backdrop for a future filmmaker. His parents were both able storytellers, regaling him with vivid tales of their experiences in World War II back in England. His father had worked for the Royal Army Ordnance Corps, where he'd repaired and maintained everything from weaponry and ammunition to uniforms and more. His mother also had stories to share, as she'd helped the war effort by building airplanes and munitions for the famed de Havilland Aircraft Company. As a result, young Peter was fascinated with war tales, and was particularly respectful of the sacrifices that had been made by the Allies to assure victory against Hitler's Germany and Hirohito's Japan.

A Director in the Making

Peter Jackson's first contact with the industry that would make him famous was an afternoon spent at a movie theater when he was about six or seven watching a special screening of an old 1957 film called *Noddy in Toyland*. Noddy, the main character, was the creation of a children's author named Enid Blyton, and the story was originally intended as a stage production. *Noddy in Toyland* was little more than the filmed version of a play.

For the most part, the film was disliked by critics and audiences. Peter, however, was enthralled by the whole experience of being able to escape the "real" world for an hour or two and be carried off into one of fantasy and fascination. Each subsequent visit to the movies simply added to his enthusiasm and his curiosity. When Jackson saw things on the screen that seemed impossible in reality, he began to understand the concept of special effects—and he wondered if he could create his own.

When his parents bought their first television in the mid 1960s—a basic black-and-white model— Peter was equally excited. To him, it was akin to having a personal movie theater. He and his father would watch it together, enjoying war movies as well as television shows such as *Monty Python's Flying Circus*.

Peter also developed a fondness for action programs aimed at youngsters, with one of his favorites being a show called *Thunderbirds*. Filmed between 1964 and 1966, *Thunderbirds* focused

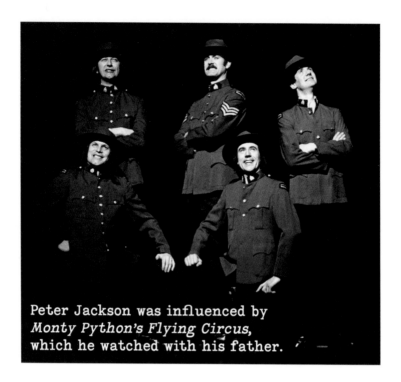

Peter Jackson was influenced by
Monty Python's Flying Circus,
which he watched with his father.

on the Tracy family, the force behind International Rescue, a top-secret organization that fights crime. It was produced using marionette puppetry and scale-model special effects, a technique dubbed "Supermarionation." Jackson and his friends would reenact scenes from the series in their backyards using their own toys or building simple props. Although the special effects in *Thunderbirds* were very crude by today's standards, they were considered a big deal among children in the 1960s, and they stirred Jackson's desire to see if it was possible to come up with a few of his own. Jackson was also intrigued by the show's use of marionettes as characters, and would later use puppetry in his own work.

As luck would have it, the Jackson family received one of the earliest compact eight-millimeter cameras available in 1971 as a gift from

MONTY PYTHON'S FLYING CIRCUS

The television show that Peter Jackson and his father most enjoyed watching together was the now-legendary *Monty Python's Flying Circus*. This sketch comedy program from England aired from 1969 to 1974, and captured the spirit of the time with its fresh and irreverent humor.

The material was often highly cerebral in nature—most of the Python members were educated in England's finest schools—which risked alienating the average viewer. But the cast compensated for this with silliness, slapstick, and satire, plus—most importantly to Jackson—an occasional foray into the vulgar, boorish, and rude. Blood, snot, vomit— nothing was off-limits in the world of Monty Python, and young Peter Jackson discovered he had a love for both comedy and all things gross and graphic. "Because I saw the *Flying Circus* at just the right age," Jackson was quoted as saying in David Konow's *Reel Terror*, "I was 11 or 12 years old and just starting to form adult sensibilities—it had a profound influence on the way in which my sense of humour developed." This would figure prominently in some of his earliest productions, particularly the dark humor in his films *Bad Taste* and *Meet the Feebles*.

This 8 mm camera is similar to the one Peter Jackson used in his earliest filmmaking efforts.

a neighbor—around the time that Peter's desire to make his own films was starting to blossom. He was about nine years old at this point, and the camera was intended for his parents as a way of chronicling family outings, parties, and other events. However, it wasn't long before Peter took ownership of it to aid his growing ambition. As Jackson later stated in an Academy of Achievement online interview in 2006, "I grabbed the camera immediately, because I thought, 'God, now I can get my spaceships that I've made, my models, and I can film them, just like *Thunderbirds.*'" Surprisingly, his parents did not seem to mind.

In fact, Jackson would later say that his parents never discouraged him from his filmmaking interests, in spite of the fact that there wasn't a robust movie industry in New Zealand, and thus no solid job opportunities for someone with his aspirations. He has stated on many occasions that their ongoing support, especially during these early years, was critical to his later success. As Jackson once said in an online interview, "I wanted to make movies and to make monsters and all this. And my parents... who were [just] very gentle, simple, conservative people... they kept trying to prod me into an architecture career, but nonetheless, every single thing I did with film, they supported me."

With family camera in hand, Peter began shooting his first amateur productions. He would gather friends to act out little dramas, with a particular focus on World War II reenactments, some of which were based on stories he'd heard from his parents and other relatives. He was primarily interested in creating whatever type of special effects he could manage, which were usually something along the lines of stop-motion animation. Stop-motion animation entails setting up figures, taking a shot, then moving those figures slightly, taking another shot, and repeating the process until you have a full sequence of events that appears on the finished film as normal motion. In this way, inanimate objects such as dinosaur models can appear as though they are fighting, or real people can look as if they are doing unusual things like sliding across the ground without actually moving their feet.

It was around this time that Jackson also encountered two movies that would have a tremendous influence on his future work. The first

Planet of the Apes showed Peter Jackson that realism could get audiences to accept implausible situations.

movie was 1933's *King Kong*, the story of a giant gorilla who is discovered on a remote island by a film crew who use him in their movie. Kong falls in love with the film's leading lady and saves her from imminent danger, only to be captured by the crew and brought back to New York City to promote their film. In one of the most famous scenes in film history, the gorilla falls to his death from the top of the Empire State Building after again saving the woman he loves. Although the special effects, particularly the stop-motion animation, are crude by today's standards, they held nine-year-old Peter Jackson spellbound. He spent many hours trying to recreate *King Kong*'s stop-motion effects using his own simple home equipment—never dreaming that, as an adult, he would go on to direct a successful remake of the film.

The other film to have a profound impact on Jackson, 1968's *Planet of the Apes*, stirred his appreciation for the dramatic impact of carefully rendered makeup and costumes. The whole premise of the movie seems ridiculous even today—in a world where ape-like creatures with human qualities are the dominant species, mankind is the inferior race. Still, the movie was a blockbuster, and young Peter believed this was because the ape characters looked incredibly real—exactly the way apes that had evolved to the point of being almost human would look—which helped to sell the premise to audiences.

Early Attempts

Peter was a good-but-not-great student with a particular strength in mathematics. As he entered his teens, his interest in filmmaking grew to such intensity that it essentially blotted out any enthusiasm he might have had for school.
His parents were always supportive of his interest in movies, but they hoped he would pursue a "proper" degree, just in case his dream of a career in film didn't work out. Nevertheless, Jackson's mind drifted during classes, and when he wasn't there, he and his friends could be found working on his latest production.

In 1978, he got wind of an amateur film contest that was sponsored throughout New Zealand schools by a television program called *Spot On*. Armed with a much-improved camera (thanks to his parents' ongoing generosity), Peter decided to take a shot at first prize. He combined the acting talents of both his friends and himself with meticulously crafted stop-motion animation to produce *The Valley*—a story about a small band of prospectors who, while searching for gold, stumble into a separate dimension of reality populated by a variety of bizarre creatures. He cleverly intercut fight sequences between the film's actors and the models he used for the creatures, and his attempt at this sort of special effect came across fairly convincingly.

Although *The Valley* did not even place in the *Spot On* contest—it was almost a half hour long, while the contest rules called for a running time of around five minutes—Peter did receive numerous compliments from the judges on what was obviously a very impressive effort by someone so young. Further, scenes from *The Valley* were aired on television nationwide in New Zealand. The film also won a smaller contest run by one of the local newspapers, which earned Jackson $100.

Not long after the hype from *The Valley* began to simmer down, Peter was faced with a big life decision. Having finished his high school education, he had to choose whether or not to go on to university. He already knew his parents' preference—they had dreams of him becoming an architect—but he also believed enough in his own budding talent to take a bold step. At the age of sixteen, he left school altogether and entered the working world. In a 2006 online interview, Jackson recalled, "I just wanted to get out of school as fast as I could, not because I hated school [but] because I wanted to buy a 16 millimeter camera... I got a job at a newspaper as a photo lithographer, and during that seven years I was there, I basically spent two of the years saving up for a 16 mm camera, which cost several thousand dollars... I lived at home with my parents all this time because I couldn't afford not to."

He tried at first to find work in film, but there really wasn't a film industry at the time in New Zealand. So, he applied for a job at a local newspaper called the *Evening Post* as a photographic lithographer. A photographic lithographer prepares plates for the printing of newspapers. While Jackson had no experience with this type of work, his personality and enthusiasm carried him through the interview, and he was given the job.

He had to travel to Auckland to train for his new position, and the commute took several hours by train each way. To keep his mind occupied during the trip, he began reading J. R. R. Tolkien's massive trilogy, *The Lord of the Rings*—the story that Peter would one day turn into one of the most successful film franchises in history. He would later say that, while reading it, he could envision turning the tale into a great movie.

Although Jackson was not particularly interested in photographic lithography, he was happy to finally be making some money, and was ready to put it back into his filmmaking. He invested in increasingly better equipment, including some that gave him the ability to add sound to his features, which he hadn't been able to do previously. During the weekends, he continued his experiments in stop-motion animation, different perspectives, homemade props and costumes, and simple special effects, pushing his creativity to the limit.

In 1978, he also fell in love with another film series—the James Bond franchise—and tried to replicate some of the Bond flavor in his own productions. This included using Morris Minor cars like the one used in the 1965 Bond film, *Thunderball*.

Peter Jackson uses the same Morris Minor cars that appear in the 1965 James Bond film, *Thunderball*.

Onward and Upward

In the early 1980s, he took another shot at a coherent, plot-based film. *The Curse of the Gravewalker* was as Gothic as the title suggests. It featured Peter not just as the film's **director** but also as its hero, a killer of the undead, while friends played vampires and other zombie-type creatures. Graves were dug in the Jackson family garden, masks were made from plaster of Paris, and smoke came courtesy of dry ice. In spite of spending weeks on the project, Jackson felt the results were disappointing—he still wasn't working with equipment that was equal to capturing his creative vision.

Badly in need of some encouragement and inspiration, he took a trip to the United States and went to the greatest movie town in the world—Hollywood. After visiting several **sets** and talking with a few industry insiders, he returned to New Zealand more determined than ever to make film creation his life's work. He took his life savings and bought a Bolex 16 mm camera—a real filmmaker's tool, at long last—and set about putting together his most ambitious project yet.

The lure of Hollywood's film industry drew Peter Jackson for an introductory visit.

2 THE PROFESSIONAL

Who Says *Bad Taste* Can't Be Good?

Armed with some more professional equipment at last, Jackson focused on putting together something more polished than the rough-and-tumble short films he'd been making. He needed to create something that demonstrated his instincts, increasingly refined skills, and growing experience that he could use as a kind of cinemagraphic calling card and, hopefully, elevate himself to the next level. Another motivator was the unsettling realization that raw film for a 16 mm camera was very expensive, so taking a casual, on-the-fly attitude toward production was no longer an option. If he was going to invest considerable money in shooting, he had to produce something worthwhile. Little did he know that this next effort would open the door to the kind of career that previously only existed in his dreams.

One of the keys to Peter Jackson's early success was his dogged determination.

The film was initially titled *Roast of the Day*, and was the story of a man who travels to a coastal town in search of food-charity donations and ends up becoming the meal—the 'roast of the day'—for a group of cannibalistic aliens. Once again, Peter enlisted friends to serve as actors, while keeping a few choice roles for himself.

Shooting began in October 1983, and there was no formal **script** *per se*—he went about filming the scenes as he envisioned them in his mind. While his original plan was to make a short film about ten to fifteen minutes long, it gradually grew in length. Jackson would fend off the boredom at his job during the week by daydreaming about what improvements could be made to the film each weekend.

Soon he and his friends were filming in different **locations**, including a handsome old home called the Gear Homestead (thanks to the help of Jackson's father, who knew the managers of the historic site). The story was expanded to include that the aliens were planning to use Earth as a kind of fast-food stopover (with humans as featured items on the menu), and that the military became involved in trying to stop them. Also, the film's title changed to *Giles' Big Day*, as the story's protagonist was named Giles Copeland.

Peter worked tirelessly on *Giles' Big Day* for years, pouring more of his earnings into every facet of its production. He built props and camera accessories, baked latex masks in his mother's oven, and recruited more friends to become on-the-spot actors as the list of characters grew. Many of the people involved have since said they were impressed by the way Jackson handled his duties. Under ordinary circumstances, he was viewed as a quiet, somewhat shy, and relatively affable

Peter Jackson built on his reputation for making splatter films in 1992 with *Braindead*.

individual—but as a director he took clear command of every situation, exhibiting focus, tremendous attention to detail, and boundless patience when problems arose. He also had an innate talent for motivating his cast and crew. He was always happy to listen to other people's ideas, and never let his ego make him feel threatened or offended by what others had to say about the project. Years later, when Peter Jackson became one of the most successful directors in the world, those who worked for him would happily report the same impressions.

Peter realized he had to stop shooting scenes for *Giles' Big Day* and cut all the footage he'd accumulated down to a manageable, reasonable length. As Jackson remembered in an online interview, "I got a very simple **editing** machine [and] I sat on my mum's kitchen table... for two weeks, I just simply edited the film that we had been shooting over the course of the last few years...

I'd been completely thinking short film, short film, and I [realized], 'My God, I'm actually making a feature film!'"

At this point, Jackson discarded the idea of producing a short piece that could be submitted to film festivals. Instead, he would add a bit more to the plot and create a feature-length movie. There was one small problem, however—he was still working at the newspaper, but earning what he needed to finish the film was proving to be painfully slow, and Peter Jackson was a young man in a hurry. He also didn't want to ask his parents or his friends for further support, considering how much they were all doing for him already.

Refusing to Give Up

Jackson's best option was to contact an entity known as the New Zealand Film Commission (NZFC). The NZFC, a government body that had been founded ten years earlier by a man named Jim Booth, produces films that exemplified and contributed to the culture of New Zealand. Aware that he was investing the New Zealand citizens' tax dollars into these films, Booth wanted to make sure the NZFC supported and turned out profitable material.

Jackson contacted Booth in January 1985 to ask for the funds needed to complete *Giles' Big Day*. He sent a videotape of what he had accomplished thus far, accompanied by an almost twenty-page letter explaining the situation, as well as a meticulous description of the movie's plotline. Peter also went into some detail about himself, and he did so in a way that was supremely confident without coming across as arrogant.

While Jim Booth was impressed by Jackson's dedication and ambition, he did not feel *Giles' Big Day* had the potential to become profitable, and he said so in a letter to Jackson about a month and a half later. Jackson was deeply disappointed by this rejection, but he was smart enough to let a little time pass and let his emotions settle before writing back. When he did, he was not shy in voicing his opinion that a terrible mistake had been made—a very bold position for someone so young and inexperienced. When Jim sent back his reply to this second letter, he restated that the NZFC could not give Jackson the financial aid he was requesting. However, he also said he was willing to have a look at *Giles' Big Day* when it was complete—at which time, just maybe, he and the Commission could do something to help.

Jackson would later say that Jim Booth's refusal to grant him any funding turned out to be a blessing in disguise, as it forced him to refine numerous details that made the film much better. He also decided to rename it *Bad Taste,* the title it would be released under.

He caught another unlikely break around this time, too. He wore a homemade gorilla suit to work one day, purely for the fun of scaring a few people around the office, and a picture of him in the suit appeared in the newspaper. This caught the attention of one of the people who worked on the New Zealand television program *Worzel Gummidge Down Under.* Impressed by Jackson's creativity, the **producers** of the show invited him to build a few small props for the series.

Peter was, of course, thrilled at this first opportunity to interact with the real film business. He was invited to the set of the show, where word quickly got around that he was making a film of his own. When they asked to see it, the professionals could see Jackson's talent shining through his lack of proper resources. Jackson told them of his struggles to get Jim Booth and the NZFC to give him funding, and they urged him to keep trying. With their encouragement, Peter Jackson took a leap of faith and showed his improved version to Jim Booth.

After seeing the latest version of the film, Booth decided it was time to get the Commission behind *Bad Taste*, and after more shoots (this time with better everything—effects, lighting, sound, costumes, props), it was finally ready. It debuted at the 1987 Cannes Film Festival, where the rights to show it in theaters were purchased by over thirty countries, making it the most successful film ever made in New Zealand up to that point. While it was considered by many to be little more than an over-the-top splatter flick, *Bad Taste* accomplished what Jackson had hoped all along—it launched his career in the film business.

Bigger and Better Things

Peter's next film project stayed in line with his love for the darkly comic, introducing the world to a group of Muppet-like creatures called Feebles— except that these characters were a bit more susceptible to the foibles and follies of human nature than the lighthearted cast of Jim Henson's Muppets. In *Meet the Feebles*, the characters in question form a theater group in search of a deal for their own television program. However, their intense personality flaws ultimately prove to be their undoing, with a climactic scene featuring the cast's diva-like leading lady, Heidi the Hippo, taking

Meet the Feebles is populated by unsavory characters, such as the one above.

weapon in hand and shooting down most of her colleagues.

The original plan for *Meet the Feebles* was, in fact, to turn it into a TV show, but when that fell through, it was rewritten into a full-length feature film. In terms of funding, Jackson was now dealing with numbers well beyond anything he'd known before—the budget ran about three-quarters of a million dollars (still considered low within the context of the film industry), two-thirds of which would be covered by the NZFC. Sadly, Jackson's relationship with the Commission would begin to sour during the film's production due to a variety of disagreements.

Meet the Feebles was released in New Zealand in December of 1989, and was then picked up in various European nations in the early '90s (it did not see a U.S. release until 1995). It received generally

NEW ZEALAND POWER COUPLE

TITLE
DIRECTOR
CAMERA

DATE   **SCENE**   **TAKE**

Just as he seems to have a natural intuition about choosing his cast and crew, Peter Jackson apparently has the same talent regarding his personal relationships. He and Frances Rosemary Walsh, his life partner and artistic collaborator, seem perfectly suited for each other—so much so that those who've worked with them often say they seem to be two bodies sharing the same mind. As Jackson put it in a 2013 interview, "Fran does an enormous amount of work that I can't do. She's a producer on the film as well as a writer. She's my partner in all sorts of ways. And I totally trust her instincts. Everything she chooses and decides is exactly the same as the decision I'd make. She's the only person I've ever met that I feel that safe with."

Fran's early ambitions lay in the world of fashion, but her interests gradually turned to music. She was then given the opportunity to write a television script in 1983, and did well enough that she was invited to work on similar

Fran Walsh and Peter Jackson were each awarded New Zealand's Order of Merit in 2002.

projects. She met Jackson in 1985 while working on the set of the TV show *Worzel Gummidge Down Under*, and has partnered with him on virtually every film he's done since then. Their strong friendship and working relationship gradually led them to fall in love.

Fran has also contributed to various musical **scores**, and even done some voice work, most notably as the voice of what *The Lord of the Rings* fans know as the "Nazgul scream," a high-pitched screech made by Tolkien's evil Ringwraiths. Still, she prefers to remain in the shadows and allow Peter the lion's share of their joint fame. They have two children together—a son, Billy, and a daughter, Katie.

good reviews and went on to become, much like *Bad Taste*, something of a cult classic. According to film critic James Berardinelli, *"Meet the Feebles* is for those with a strong stomach and a seriously warped sense of humor. The film is so off the beaten track that it makes *Monty Python* seem mainstream."

Peter also benefitted from the production of *Feebles* in another way—he fell in love with one of the film's co-**screenwriters**, Fran Walsh, and they forged a lasting relationship.

Returning to the splatter/horror **genre** that he loved, Jackson's next film was *Braindead*, about a town that's being overrun by zombies. After a woman is bitten by a Sumatran Rat Monkey and is turned into a zombie, she begins turning others into zombies. Meanwhile, her devoted son tries desperately to keep the situation under wraps. The film descends into a nightmare of blood and gore, furthering Jackson's reputation as a "splattermaster."

Braindead was shot with a budget of around $3 million and took roughly three months to complete. It was released in New Zealand in August 1992, then in February of 1993 in the U.S. and Australia with the title *Dead Alive*. While it did not do well at the **box office**, it was viewed favorably by most critics and won several awards. Like Jackson's other early work, *Braindead* would be embraced as a cult hit in later years.

The Road to Hollywood

For his next film, Peter went in a slightly different, but no less evocative, direction. At Fran's urging, he decided to dramatize New Zealand's infamous 1954 Parker-Hulme murder. *Heavenly Creatures* tells

Kate Winslet and Melanie Lynskey starred in
Heavenly Creatures.

the true story of two teenage girls who became
close friends and created a fictional world that
caused them to become increasingly delusional
and detached from reality. When circumstances
threatened to separate them, the two teens
murdered one of their mothers in their desperate
effort to stay together.

In spite of the controversial subject matter,
thorough research on Jackson and Fran's part, a
fairly aggressive marketing campaign, and even
an **Academy Award** nomination, the 1994 film
did poorly at the box office, failing to cover its
$5 million budget. Nevertheless, Jackson was
continuing to gain priceless experience as a writer
and director, and people within the movie business
were beginning to take notice. *Heavenly Creatures*
was also significant in that it introduced the world to
another figure in the film industry who would go on

to great success—actress Kate Winslet, who played the role of Juliet Hulme.

In 1995, Jackson released *Forgotten Silver*, a mockumentary—a satirical, tongue-in-cheek documentary—about a New Zealand filmmaker named Colin McKenzie who had significant impact on the movie business and yet was forgotten by history. In reality, McKenzie is a fictional character, and the supposedly "recently discovered" film clips in the mockumentary were all created by Jackson, who carefully mimicked the style of early cinema to make them appear authentic. Notable industry insiders such as movie critic and historian Leonard Maltin and Harvey Weinstein (a producer, business executive, and the co-founder of the entertainment company Miramax Films) make appearances in the film, as does Jackson himself. It was never given a formal theatrical release, and instead was shown on New Zealand television (where many viewers first thought it was a real documentary) and at several film festivals. Although public reaction was mixed at the time, *Forgotten Silver* has since become a favorite among Jackson's fans as well as most professional critics.

With Jackson's credibility seeming to grow by the day, he was at last given the break of a lifetime—the chance to make a big-budget Hollywood feature for **Universal Studios**. Thanks to the support of veteran film producer and director Robert Zemeckis (*Who Framed Roger Rabbit, Forrest Gump*, and the *Back to the Future* franchise), Universal even allowed Jackson to stay in New Zealand to do it, instead of insisting he shoot in the United States. That film turned out to be 1996's *The Frighteners*, a horror-comedy about an ordinary man who, following his wife's murder, acquires the ability to see and

Michael J. Fox talks with ghosts in 1996's
The Frighteners.

communicate with ghosts. The central conflict begins
when one of these spirits, a murdering lunatic when
he was mortal, begins killing again.

Peter and Fran were enthusiastic about the
script, and actor Michael J. Fox, at the height of his
popularity, played the lead character. Nevertheless,
the movie failed to perform well in theaters.
Jackson and Fran were deeply disappointed by
what many considered a second consecutive failure,
and he wondered if his career as a filmmaker was
finished. In the film industry, your track record is
everything, and Peter Jackson's was beginning to
look a little shaky.

He had no way of knowing that his next project
wouldn't just bring his career to new heights—it
would turn him into a household name.

3 ONE STORY TO RULE THEM ALL

A Rough Start

Peter Jackson had read J.R.R. Tolkien's *The Lord of the Rings* trilogy on the train to Auckland while learning the ropes as a photo lithographer. It is a mind-stretching thousand-page mega-adventure set in the world of Tolkien's intriguing Middle Earth. Every fantasy beast and being imaginable is featured in the story, from orcs and wizards and hobbits to dragons and elves and talking trees. Not long after finishing *The Frighteners*, Jackson began thinking about bringing this wondrous, many-layered epic to the silver screen. It had been done before, but only through a low-budget, animated feature that did little to convey the impact of Tolkien's dramatic vision. Now that the technology to create magnificent special effects—and tell Tolkien's tale properly—was available, Jackson couldn't understand why no one else had thought of doing it.

Peter Jackson had wanted to make a film adaptation of J. R. R. Tolkien's *Lord of the Rings* trilogy since reading the books as a teenager.

The first step to fulfilling this dream, he knew, was to secure the film rights to the books—and, as it turned out, this would become a major undertaking in itself. The person who owned those rights was the movie producer and record executive Saul Zaentz, who had produced *The Lord of the Rings* animated feature in 1978. Jackson decided to make the film with his friend Harvey Weinstein, who was the head of Miramax Films (and had appeared in Jackson's *Forgotten Silver*). To do this, they needed to work out a deal with Zaentz.

Jackson, however, suddenly became sidetracked by an unexpected opportunity—Universal Studios offered him the chance to direct a remake of his beloved *King Kong*. Unfortunately, problems quickly arose during pre-production on the project, and in 1997 Universal decided to cancel the remake. With that distraction put to rest, Jackson went back to ironing out the details concerning the *Rings* film rights.

Jackson and Fran also began putting together what would become the movie version of the trilogy. It would be easy to assume that the most logical approach to filming *The Lord of the Rings* would be to simply shoot three films—one for each part of the trilogy. However, Miramax was only able to put up the money for two. Jackson, Fran, and their team worked for months on a **treatment** that condensed the three parts of the trilogy into two films.

By 1998, Jackson and Fran had what they felt was the most reasonably "stripped down" version of Tolkien's classic story that didn't compromise his creative vision. They also realized they would need at least double the money Miramax was able to raise. Upon hearing this, Weinstein and the Miramax team decided the only way they could stay within their original budget was to trim the story down even

Philippa Boyens, Fran Walsh and Peter Jackson's long-time writing collaborator.

further into a single film—something that Jackson felt was impossible. By this time, Peter, Fran, and their writing collaborator, Philippa Boyens, had literally spent years trying to get the *Rings* project in motion. The thought of having to give it up after so much work was heartbreaking.

Feeling he had nothing to lose, Jackson shopped the project around to other studios in Hollywood. He spent a month meeting with producers, showing them a brief tape of some of the work they'd already done, as well as samples of the story treatment they'd spent so much time creating. Studio after studio turned him down, and he was beginning to grow fairly depressed. Then, at his last scheduled meeting, he sat down with the people from New Line Cinema—and they asked Jackson why he wanted to make only two films when there were three books in the series. An astonished Jackson listened as they politely explained that

The Weta Workshop in Wellington, New Zealand has achieved such renown that it warranted a visit from Britain's Prince Charles.

they were interested in backing the project, but only if Jackson was willing to shoot three films, not two.

Creating Another World

Peter, Fran, and Philippa now had to compose yet another treatment of the *Rings* story, this time dividing it again into three parts. While this meant a lot more work, it also meant much more creative freedom. When they were finished, storyboards were created. These comic book visualizations of each scene would be used as a reference by the cast and crew. Two artists—Alan Lee and John Howe, who had both previously illustrated editions of Tolkien's books—were brought in to begin conceptual design work in August of 1997.

Once the films began to shape up visually, Jackson then had to contact the right experts to turn those visions into realities. He called on a New Zealand company that specialized in the creation of props, costumes, model-making, and special effects—the famed Weta Workshop.

Having already used the company's expertise on *Meet the Feebles* and *Heavenly Creatures*, Jackson felt comfortable entrusting Weta's director, Richard Taylor, with the massive task of handling *The Lord of the Rings* trilogy. For the *Rings* films to become the definitive screen versions of Tolkien's classic books, they agreed that the key would be to make everything that fans saw on the screen appear as genuine as possible. The ultimate goal, then, would be to make someone sitting in the theater forget that they were watching events unfold in a make-believe world, and instead feel as though Middle Earth truly existed.

To achieve this, Richard and the Weta team, with input from Jackson, went about building literally thousands of props, costumes, monsters, and models. They made real swords, real armor, real arrows, real bows. They stitched miles of fabric into some of the most intricate and delicate costumes in movie history. Hairy feet were molded for the hobbits, and horrific facial prosthetics were created for the orcs and Uruk-hai. Weta spent tens of millions of dollars on their contributions to the *Rings* films, and Jackson marveled—just as the movie-going public would—at the stunning work they produced. It was a far cry from the days he spent baking latex masks in his mom's oven.

Filming began in October 1999, and Jackson, sensitive to the fact that a trilogy of this size would cost a fortune to make, decided that one way to economize would be to shoot one unbelievably long film, edit it into three separate films, and release them one at a time. This approach ensured that each installment of the trilogy would have a coherent, uniform feel. Viewers would feel they were picking up right where the story left off when they saw the second and third movie.

To make this happen, Jackson would need to plan out a very long shooting schedule. Everyone in the cast and crew would be working together for a long time, and would have to get along, much like a family. With this in mind, Peter was careful when selecting people to bring into the project. During auditions, he would have to judge not just an actor's talent but also his or her personality. He didn't want actors who were arrogant, selfish, or demanding. He searched out those who would get along with others because, for the better part of a year, that's exactly what they would have to do.

The story that would be told over the course of these three movies was that of little Frodo Baggins, a hobbit of unquestionable decency and virtue. He is given the unenviable task of having to bring the Ring of Power back to the place where it was forged—the lava-spewing Mount Doom, set in the heart of the dark kingdom of Mordor—so it can be destroyed.

Along the way, Frodo collects a group of noble allies to help him in this daunting quest. But the Ring's allure of nearly unlimited power brings out the worst in those who encounter it—and no one wants it more than the evil Sauron, who rules Mordor through fear and cruelty. Frodo has to make his way through an unknown world while dodging Sauron's many agents. To make things even more difficult for Frodo, a few of those who have sworn to protect him are also unable to resist the Ring's enchantment, and they become a danger to him as well.

Elijah Wood played the lead role of Frodo
Baggins in *The Lord of the Rings* trilogy.

The shooting schedule that would cover all three
films lasted 274 days, from October of 1999 until
December of 2000. During that period, Jackson would
film at more than 150 locations in New Zealand.
Researching, selecting, and securing every location

used in the film was a long and arduous process. In most locations, the environmental impact on the shooting area had to be minimized: Jackson would be allowed to shoot his movie only if he agreed to leave each place exactly as he'd found it. He also spent portions of 2001 to 2004 filming "pickup" scenes— relatively minor shots deemed critical to the flow of the story.

When all the filming was done, the cast got to go home—but for Jackson, the next stage of the process was just beginning. The editing for the *Rings* trilogy was to be a massive undertaking in itself, if for no other reason than he had shot more than one thousand miles of film. Peter spent months in the editing room. During this time, he also oversaw continuing work on special effects, sound, and the musical score. Jackson could have gone to Hollywood to work on all this. Instead, he stayed in the New Zealand film creation community he'd created with his Weta Workshop colleagues— "Wellywood"— the home of his production company, Wingnut Films.

Blockbusters Abound

The first film, *The Fellowship of the Ring*, hit movie theaters December 19, 2001 in more than 3,300 locations—and was met with overwhelming approval from both consumers and critics. It was praised for everything from its magnificent cast and their performances to the breathtaking costumes, convincing props, and dazzling effects. Created with a budget of just under $100 million, *Fellowship* earned nearly $900 million in box-office sales alone, making it one of the most profitable movies

The hobbit-sized sets for the *Lord of the Rings* cramped Gandalf the Wizard, played by the celebrated actor Ian McKellen.

in history. It then went on to win a staggering number of awards, including four **Oscars** (out of an incredible thirteen Oscar nominations).

Jackson had, nearly overnight, gone from being fairly well known in New Zealand for making somewhat tasteless but comical cult films to one of the most celebrated directors on the planet. *Fellowship* was his most successful attempt to reach a mainstream audience. It seemed as though every single Tolkien fan was rushing to theaters to watch this stunning masterpiece. Perhaps even more incredibly, *Fellowship* lured a slice of the public that even Jackson hadn't expected—people who had never actually read *The Lord of the Rings*.

The second film, *The Two Towers*, came out almost a year to the day after *Fellowship*, hitting theaters on December 18, 2002 (December 19 in

FINISHING A FILM

TITLE
DIRECTOR
CAMERA

DATE   SCENE   TAKE

When the cameras stop rolling and every scene has been shot, a film's creation is far from over. All of the work that happens after this stage is known as post production, and is comprised of many parts. One of the most significant is the editing process, which involves cutting down all the footage into the final version of the movie that audiences see. This is a trickier undertaking than many imagine. A great deal of time and care is taken in reviewing each version of every scene to choose the one that works best. Then, all the scenes that are chosen have to link together in a sensible way in order to tell a coherent and interesting story.

Also key to post production is the composition and performance of a film's music, also known as its score. The people who compose the scores for most movies are usually involved for just a few weeks once filming is completed, but composer Howard Shore spent three years on the *Rings* trilogy. Following the release of *The Fellowship of the Ring*, Shore said, "You have to consider this score, which is two and a half hours long, as Act One of a three-act piece. I used an opera concept to shape it because it

was the largest musical form that you could use... (*The Lord of the Rings* trilogy score is) a nine-hour piece."

A third critical component is the creation and addition of special effects. It is tricky to make those effects blend seamlessly with the actors' performances. You might be able to create a realistic dragon, but if it doesn't look as though that dragon is interacting with the human characters, it can throw off the viewer.

Peter Jackson, by insisting on creating his movies in his native New Zealand, has had to also create what had never existed there before: an actual film production industry. Wellington, New Zealand is now affectionately known as "Wellywood," and is the home of several film industry-related companies Jackson owns or co-owns an interest in: Weta Digital—the digital effects company Jackson helped build to create the effects for his films—as well as a costume and props company (Weta Workshop), a full post production facility (Park Road Post), a studio complex with four soundstages (Stone Street Studios), and an equipment rental company.

New Zealand). Picking up the story where *The Fellowship of the Ring* left off, *The Two Towers* featured a few new characters that charmed fans by the millions. One was the treacherous Gollum, whose mind had been poisoned by the Ring of Power during the time it was in his possession. He was now supposedly helping Frodo bring it back to Mount Doom, but a part of him dreamed of getting it back. Gollum was nothing more than pixels on the screen—the product of **performance-capture** technology: a live actor (in this case, Andy Serkis) performs the scene, and then that performance is transitioned into a **computer-generated image (CGI)**. Also popular with fans were the Ents—the talking, walking trees of Fangorn Forest who play an important role in helping Frodo's allies.

The Two Towers was just as well received as *Fellowship*. In fact, it did even better in terms of ticket sales, bringing in more than $925 million at the box office. *The Two Towers* was lauded by critics and audiences as a stunning (towering, you might say) cinemagraphic achievement. Once more, the awards poured in, including two Oscars out of six nominations.

The third and final film in the trilogy, *The Return of the King*, was to be Peter Jackson's crowning achievement. Released on December 17, 2003 (December 18 in New Zealand), it brought all of the existing storylines to dramatic and deeply emotional conclusions, closing off the series with a power rarely delivered in movie history. It would be viewed not just as one the finest films of that year, but one of the greatest ever.

In terms of box-office success, *The Return of the King* beat out the previous two films by earning more than $1.1 billion. Then, it stunned the film

Andy Serkis cozies up to a model of the character he helped to create, Gollum.

industry by receiving eleven Oscar nominations—including Best Director—and winning all of them. It is a record that remains unbroken.

For the once quiet and shy little boy from New Zealand, life would never be the same.

A STYLE ALL HIS OWN

Like all successful directors, Peter Jackson has his own working style. He is a tireless worker who gets up early and goes to bed late. (During the production of *Rings*, he got no more than five hours of sleep a night.) His patience and persistence are legendary among his colleagues, as is his knack for making a shoot relaxed and fun. He is often seen in a wrinkled shirt and shorts, and he seems perfectly happy to walk around barefoot most of the time (just like a hobbit).

Peter likes to play pranks on his cast and crew, and doesn't mind when they do likewise. He also doesn't mind taking suggestions from the people around him—a rare quality in a director of his stature. In the interest of making the best film possible, he is willing to set aside his own ideas if he feels a better one is available. He also has a habit of asking for repeated takes from his actors so he can shoot a scene from numerous angles. While some cast members find this tiring and even irritating, it provides Jackson with a greater selection of choices when it comes time to edit.

Peter Jackson won his first Academy Award in 2004.

4 HOLLYWOOD DARLING

The Return of a Very Different King

Following the record-breaking success of *The Lord of the Rings* films, Peter Jackson was no longer considered some small-time director from New Zealand. The keys to Hollywood were thrust in his hand—and he already knew which door he would open.

In 2003, as he was doing post production work on *Return of the King*, Universal Studios approached him about reviving the *King Kong* project. Jackson had been interested in the project the first time around, but too many snags got in the way. The situation was quite different this time, however, and he jumped on the opportunity to pay homage to one of the movies that changed his life.

Jackson still had his script from the aborted 1996 attempt, and he, Fran, and Philippa went about updating it. (The three of them had formed such a comfortable and cohesive team that they

Peter Jackson, who was enthralled by the 1933 classic *King Kong*, got to remake the movie about seventy years after the original was released.

The first *King Kong* was shot using a process known as stop-motion animation.

are now regarded within the film industry as one screenwriting entity.) He vowed to stay close to the original film from 1933 this time, and would even reinstate a few scenes that had been cut from it. Universal increased the 1996 budget from $150 million to $175 million. Jackson rehired Richard Taylor and the Weta Workshop gang, as well as most of the *Rings* crew.

In 1933, *Kong* had been the product of stop-motion animation, and while Jackson had loved this technique as a boy, he knew it simply wouldn't work for the modern market. He realized that filming the character of Kong would be best accomplished through performance-capture technology.

PETER JACKSON

Once again, Peter turned to someone he knew and trusted, and asked actor Andy Serkis to play Kong. Serkis, who had dazzled the world with his portrayal of Gollum in *Rings*, had set the bar awfully high, and he wanted his Kong to be no less brilliant.

It was important to both him and Jackson that Kong did not appear too human (or, even worse, like a human in a gorilla costume), so Serkis wanted to research the subject firsthand. He began by visiting London Zoo in his native England, where he watched four gorillas as they interacted with each other in their enclosures. This visit proved disappointing, however, because gorillas in captivity have lost a bit of their 'edge' and behave differently than those in the wild. So, Serkis traveled to Rwanda, where he observed gorillas in their natural habitat. He especially wanted to see how they communicated through expression and body language because, unlike Gollum, Kong would have no lines.

"They kept you on your toes," Serkis would later report about the experience during an interview for the magazine *Total Film*, "because they were all around you. I didn't actually know that they weren't going to charge us, because one or two did charge us. But, on the whole, I felt fairly safe."

Filming began in September of 2004, and once again Jackson decided to stage the entire production in New Zealand. Most of the shooting took place on studio sets in "Wellywood," but a few scenes were shot on location in Auckland and Wellington. At one point the film began to go past its budget, and Universal executives became concerned. Jackson showed them what had been done up to that point, and they agreed to raise the funding once more, this time to just over $200 million—making *Kong* one of the most expensive films in history.

King Kong was released in December of 2005 and, while it did not pile up the galactic numbers of *The Lord of the Rings* films, it still earned more than half a billion dollars in theaters. Some industry insiders viewed the film as a mild disappointment after the *Rings* trilogy, but *Kong* was a very different kind of film and should be enjoyed on its own merits. Jackson would talk about the differences in making *Kong* in a 2005 interview: "We had layers of complication on *Kong* when we were in the cutting room that we never had on *The Lord Of The Rings* films. For any scene with *Kong* in it, we had to not only look at all the footage that we shot on set, we had to look at all of Andy Serkis' motion capture footage for the body movements, which he might have done 20 or 25 takes for, and then a separate capture for his facial expressions, so there might be another 25 takes of that." All of that effort paid off, as *King Kong* went on to win three Academy Award awards (out of four nominations).

Little Girl Lost

For his next project, Jackson ventured into the paranormal with a filmed version of Alice Sebold's 2002 bestseller, *The Lovely Bones*. It's the heartbreaking, strangely touching story of a fourteen-year-old Pennsylvania girl who is murdered by a neighbor. She remains in a kind of limbo between heaven and Earth in order to protect her family and attempt to bring her killer to justice. In time, she learns that the killer has murdered other young girls, whom she meets and befriends in their haunting "in-between" world.

The story had caught the interest of famed director Steven Spielberg in 2003, but he decided not to acquire the rights. Jackson acquired them in early 2004, and a short time later he, Fran, and Philippa began transitioning the book into a screenplay. They were also busy with both *Rings* and *King Kong*, and it took a few years to finish the script.

Saoirse Ronan attracted Peter Jackson's attention with her performance as Briony Tallis in 2007's *Atonement*.

Finally, in mid 2007, a studio decided to finance the project—and that studio, ironically, was Steven Spielberg's DreamWorks. Shooting began that fall, and this time Jackson was lured out of New Zealand, filming some scenes in both Pennsylvania and Delaware. For the crucial lead role, he cast thirteen-year-old New York actress Saoirse Ronan, who had already stunned audiences with her performance in 2007's *Atonement*, for which she became one of the youngest women ever to receive an Academy Award nomination for Best Supporting Actress.

The film hit theaters in December of 2009 and was not as warmly received as Jackson's other productions. It was generally agreed that the camera and special effects work met Jackson's usual high standards, but the storytelling was uneven in some places, and some critics blamed the quality of the screenplay. In spite of these difficulties, the film did manage to make a small profit—it earned just under $100 million. While Saoirse Ronan did win several awards for her solid performance, the film was generally overlooked at the Oscars, receiving just one nomination.

Sharing the Glory

Shaking off the tepid reaction to *The Lovely Bones*, Jackson next got involved with a movie aimed at a younger audience called *The Adventures of Tintin*. While working with DreamWorks on *The Lovely Bones*, Jackson and Steven Spielberg found they had a lot in common, including a love of the original *Tintin* comic books. When Spielberg decided to turn *Tintin* into a film, he realized that some of it should be shot through live-performance capture— something he hadn't worked much with before. So, he brought Jackson on board to co-direct and co-produce the movie, which revolves around a young boy, Tintin, and his attempts to keep the whereabouts of a once-lost treasure from the evil villain Sakharine.

Peter Jackson and Steven Spielberg collaborated on *Tintin* in 2011.

Jackson and Spielberg began filming in early 2009 in a somewhat unusual but entirely modern method of production. Jackson co-directed the first week's shooting on-site, then headed back to New Zealand. He then supervised the rest of the shooting through videoconferencing, while Spielberg remained on set. Numerous actors came in to try their hand at live-performance capture, including Jamie Bell in the lead role of Tintin, and James Bond actor Daniel Craig as Sakharine. Andy Serkis, by this time probably the best-known performance-capture actor in the world, played the role of Haddock.

Post production on Tintin was crucial to the film's success, and Jackson took the helm with the aid of the Weta team. Ever the innovators, the Weta Digital staff designed new software to add greater realism to the lighting that appeared in Tintin's computer-generated world. Spielberg supervised the post production process from the United States through videoconferencing, just as Jackson had done during the shoot.

The Adventures of Tintin hit theaters in December of 2011, and was received positively by both movie fans and critics. Many compared it to Spielberg's smash 1981 success *Raiders of the Lost Ark* in terms of sheer entertainment value. In spite of the film's monster budget of nearly $120 million, it earned back more than three times that through the box office. *The Adventures of Tintin* won its share of awards as well, although it received just one Oscar nomination. In 2012, Jackson announced that there would be at least one more *Tintin* adventure, or perhaps two, and that he was interested in taking on the director's duties when the time came.

However, as all Peter Jackson fans already knew, he had something else to do first.

A BOY AT HEART

Along with fame and success, Jackson has also enjoyed tremendous wealth in his career. Although he lives comfortably, he seems at heart to be the same little boy who sat mesmerized while watching *King Kong* and *The Planet of the Apes*.

He enjoys the moviemaking process as much as ever, and clearly does it for personal satisfaction more than profit. He has used some of his money to support charitable causes, including stem cell research and the preservation of significant historical sites in his native New Zealand, particularly in the Wellington area. He has also indulged in a few lifelong fantasies, including a collection of vintage airplanes.

He has not forgotten what it was like to struggle in his early days, either. He has given both time and funding to aid several talented young filmmakers in his home country. With that kind of support and encouragement, one of them just might turn out to be the next Peter Jackson.

5 HERE AND BACK AGAIN

Another Rocky Road

The reason J. R. R. Tolkien wrote *The Lord of the Rings* books was to follow up on the worldwide popularity of his first Middle Earth book, *The Hobbit*. It is the tale of little Bilbo Baggins, who loves the quiet, rural life. Bilbo is pulled into an adventurous quest by a band of dwarves who must slay a mighty dragon named Smaug to reclaim the mountain home of their people. Bilbo returns home with a portion of Smaug's massive hoard of gold as a reward.

The Hobbit was published in 1937 and was intended merely as a children's fantasy tale, but it eventually drew a much bigger following. Tolkien, a university professor, would later confess that he began the story with just one line—"In a hole in the ground there lived a hobbit"—and from there let his imagination lead him. He had the first draft finished in 1932, and in 1936 it was accepted for publication

The crew began preparing
sets for *The Hobbit* trilogy
a year before filming began.

by Stanley Unwin, founder and director of the publishing house George Allen & Unwin.

When the book was released in 1937 it was an immediate success, leading Unwin to ask Tolkien for more Middle Earth stories. Tolkien then went about writing the three books that would form *The Lord of the Rings*. The *Rings* series would be a bit darker and more graphic (Tolkien probably did not intend them for young children, as *The Hobbit* had been). Nevertheless, the *Rings* trilogy became just as successful, ensuring Tolkien's place in literary history.

Peter Jackson was always interested in filming both *The Hobbit* and *The Lord of the Rings*. However, when he began pursuing the rights to both books back in the mid 1990s, he hit a snag. Saul Zaentz owned all the *Rings* rights, as well as the production rights to *The Hobbit*. However, a film studio called United Artists owned a different set of rights for *The Hobbit* known as distribution rights. Jackson wasn't able to make a deal with United Artists at the time, and decided to move forward with just the *Rings* stories instead.

In late 2007, all conflicts were settled, and it was announced that Jackson would be involved with *The Hobbit*—but only as its executive producer, not its director. In early 2008, it was announced that filmmaker Guillermo del Toro would direct instead. The Mexican-born del Toro would also be involved in the screenwriting of *The Hobbit*, which would be two films rather than one (even though there was only one *Hobbit* book).

Eager to begin, del Toro jumped right into the fray. He met with the Weta people to discuss early ideas for visual elements, and held long writing sessions with Jackson, Walsh, and Boyens. While it appeared that all parties were getting along very

Guillermo del Toro pulled out as director of *The Hobbit* trilogy when financial problems hit MGM.

well, there were rumblings in the fan community that nothing short of a Peter Jackson–directed version of *The Hobbit* would be satisfactory. However, Jackson stated he wasn't willing to make such a massive sacrifice of time and energy again (the *Rings* movies had consumed ten years of his life). The fans, it appeared, would have to accept the fact that Jackson felt del Toro would be just as good.

Ironically, an unforeseen negative turned into a positive for Jackson's fans. Metro-Goldwyn-Mayer (MGM), which had purchased United Artists, began having serious financial difficulties in the mid 2000s. By the end of the decade it had filed for bankruptcy, and all projects were put on hold. The possibility of the company being sold off, either whole or in pieces, meant that the future of the *Hobbit* films was in serious question. In light of this, Guillermo del Toro decided in the spring of 2010 to leave *The Hobbit* in order to work on other films. The following summer, Jackson took the director's chair.

SIR PETER

Jackson receiving the Insignia of the Order of New Zealand from Governor-General Sir Jerry Mateparae in 2013.

In September of 2013, Peter Jackson received the Insignia of the Order of New Zealand, his nation's highest honor. This came three years after he was made a Knight Companion of the New Zealand Order of Merit by the Nation's Governor-General, Anand Satyanand. This was in recognition of his services to the arts, which bolstered New Zealand's film industry and boosted its tourism trade. Many people decided to visit the country because of the breathtaking scenery depicted in his films. This wasn't Jackson's first such honor—in 2002, he received the Companion of the New Zealand Order of Merit, which is ranked just below knighthood.

Return to Middle Earth

Once Jackson took the helm of *The Hobbit*, the wheels really began turning in every area. Locations were scouted, the Weta gang began working on everything from props to costumes to models, and word came down that MGM would most likely emerge from its bankruptcy stronger than ever and be able to continue as planned. In the autumn of 2010, Jackson got busy with what he knew would be one of the keys to making *The Hobbit* films work—casting.

Many of the stars that appeared in the *Rings* films were approached to see if they'd be interested in reprising their roles, but it was a tricky situation. In the original novels, the events of *The Hobbit* occurred about sixty years before those in the *Rings* trilogy, which meant that some *Rings* characters, in spite of being enormously popular with fans, simply do not appear in *The Hobbit* at all. How could their appearance in the *Hobbit* films be justified? Jackson, Walsh, and Boyens decided it would be possible to incorporate them in some instances with the use of flashback sequences. A few actors whose characters fell into this group did agree to make *Hobbit* appearances, such as Elijah Wood in the role of Frodo Baggins. Others, such as Viggo Mortensen who played Aragorn, decided not to return.

Then there were those characters who were legitimately in both *The Hobbit* and *The Lord of the Rings* books, such as the elven Lord Elrond and the old wizard Gandalf. Fortunately, the actors who played them in *Rings* were still available and willing to take on these parts once again. Even

Andy Serkis, playing the frightful Gollum, came back to get into his performance-capture gear again. He would also have expanded duties this time as **second-unit director**.

For the newer roles exclusive to *The Hobbit*, Jackson followed the same stringent criteria as he did with *Rings*. For the young Bilbo Baggins, he cast Martin Freeman, a well-established English actor who had already earned legions of fans in such roles as Dr. Watson in the television series *Sherlock*. For the critical role of dwarf leader Thorin Oakenshield, Jackson chose Richard Armitage, who was excellent as Guy of Gisborne in the BBC television production of *Robin Hood*. Since the fearsome dragon Smaug would be walking and talking like any other character, Peter tapped Martin Freeman's colleague from *Sherlock*, the acclaimed actor Benedict Cumberbatch, for the role.

Filming began in March 2011 in New Zealand. A farm in the rural town of Matamata had been the setting for the hobbit village of Hobbiton in *Rings*, and was "recycled" for *The Hobbit*. To give the area complete authenticity, designers began building hobbit dwellings and planting flowers more than a year before *The Hobbit* shoot began.

As with *Rings*, the shooting schedule for *The Hobbit* was long and arduous, lasting more than 260 days. When it was finished in July of 2012, Jackson decided he would further divide *The Hobbit* into a third film, making it a trilogy just like *Rings*. Thus, more shooting had to be undertaken in May of 2013, which lasted for just over two months.

The first of the *Hobbit* films, titled *An Unexpected Journey*, was released on December 14, 2012, and was an immediate hit with movie fans. Box office receipts exceeded the $1 billion mark worldwide.

Some viewers, however, were not as ebullient about *An Unexpected Journey* as they'd been with the *Rings* films. Jackson, Walsh, and Boyens exercised some creative license in order to straddle *The Hobbit* over three films—which, in itself, seemed an example of crass commercialism to some fans. A few reviewers also took exception to the changes that were made from Tolkien's original vision.

The second *Hobbit* film, *The Desolation of Smaug*, was released one year later almost to the day of the first—December 13, 2013. Again, most consumers and critics reacted positively. Some even stated that they felt this second film was a bit better than the first, particularly in terms of pace.

Jackson had expected this reaction, since it had been necessary to include moments of exposition into *An Unexpected Journey*, which slowed its pace a little. While this exposition material didn't necessarily move *An Unexpected Journey*'s story forward in terms of action or development, it did introduce and set up characters and other details for maximum impact in the other two films. Because of it, *The Desolation of Smaug* moves along more quickly, with numerous action sequences that build on the first film and set up the viewer for the third.

The third and final *Hobbit* film, titled *The Battle of the Five Armies*, was scheduled for release on December 17, 2014.

The Future

For a man like Peter Jackson, the journey will likely never end. He has already made an indelible mark on film history, and he certainly has earned more money than he could spend in ten lifetimes.

CAMEOS ABOUND

Jackson and daughter Katie together on the red carpet.

Peter Jackson has appeared on screen, albeit in various roles and costumes, in nearly all of his films. In the first *Hobbit* movie, he played a dwarf who flees during an attack by Smaug the dragon. In the second, he played a slovenly resident of the town of Bree—the same role he played in *The Fellowship of the Ring*.

He rarely has had speaking roles, however, preferring to leave the real acting to others. As he has become more successful and more famous, he has also shown up in the work of other directors, such as the feature film *Hot Fuzz* by Edgar Wright and the made-for-TV movie *The Five(ish) Doctors Reboot* by Jackson Davison.

On a family note, Fran Walsh had a brief appearance in *The Lovely Bones*, and both of their children, Billy and Katie, have been on screen in almost every movie they've made.

Peter Jackson wants to push the limits of technology.

Why does he still do it? For the same reason he did as a boy who spent every penny he earned on one more roll of film, or one more batch of plaster of Paris so he could make horror masks in his mother's oven—because he loves it. In particular, he seems eternally fascinated by the latest developments in filmmaking technology and what new frontiers they will enable him to explore. As he stated in an interview with the quarterly magazine of the Director's Guild of America:

> I've asked myself, 'In a hundred years' time, is film going to look like it does now?' And I think the chances of that are incredibly small. Somewhere between now and the next hundred-year mark, people should be experimenting, using technology to push things forward, trying to break out. [D]o you try to use technology to improve the audience experience? That's what I'm interested in. I've got no great nostalgic desire to preserve the look of film. Anything we can do with ever-evolving technology to actually immerse people in the entertainment experience is something we should all be trying to do.

FILMOGRAPHY

The following is a list of the films Peter Jackson has either directed, written, produced, served as executive producer, or acted in as of 2014.
The films are listed in alphabetical order by year.
For a complete listing, please visit the Internet Movie Database website, www.IMDb.com.

The Valley (1976 / director, writer, producer, actor)

Bad Taste (1987 / director, writer, producer, actor)

Meet the Feebles (1989 / director, writer, producer, actor)

Dead Alive (released as *Braindead* in New Zealand) (1992 / director, writer, actor)

Valley of the Stereos (1992 / executive producer)

Heavenly Creatures (1994 / director, writer, producer, actor)

Forgotten Silver (1995 / director, writer, executive producer, actor)

Jack Brown Genius (1996 / writer, producer)

The Frighteners (1996 / director, writer, producer, actor)

The Lord of the Rings: The Fellowship of the Ring (2001 / director, writer, producer, actor)

The Lord of the Rings: The Two Towers (2002 / director, writer, producer, actor)

The Lord of the Rings: The Return of the King (2003 / director, writer, executive producer, actor)

The Long and Short of It (2003 / executive producer, actor)

King Kong (2005 / director, writer, producer, actor)

Hot Fuzz (2007 / actor)

Crossing the Line (2008 / director, writer)

District 9 (2009 / producer)

The Lovely Bones (2009 / director, writer, producer, actor)

The Adventures of Tintin: The Secret of the Unicorn (2011 / director, producer)

West of Memphis (2012 / producer)

The Hobbit: An Unexpected Journey (2012 / director, writer, producer, actor)

The Hobbit: The Desolation of Smaug (2013 / director, writer, producer, actor)

The Hobbit: The Battle of the Five Armies (2014 / director, writer, producer, actor)

GLOSSARY

Academy Award—Award of excellence given to a film and/or its cast and crew by the Academy of Motion Picture Arts and Sciences. Also commonly called an "Oscar."

box office—The place where money is collected before people go into a movie theater.

computer-generated imagery (CGI)—Images, both still and moving, created with the aid of computers and then used in a movie.

director—The person who oversees the shooting of a movie.

edit—To organize scenes from a film after it has been shot in order to tell a coherent story.

genre—A category of artistic work, *e.g.*, comedy, drama, Western, sci-fi, etc.

location—A place in the "real world" where a movie is shot, as opposed to a set created in a studio lot and then disassembled afterward.

Oscar—Another name for an Academy Award.

performance-capture—Shooting the movements of a real actor, then turning that performance into CGI imagery.

producer—The organizer and general manager of a movie's production.

score—The music written for a movie.

screenwriter—A person who writes the script for a movie.

script—A multi-page document outlining the scenes, dialog, emotions, and other details of a movie.

second-unit director—Someone who directs the shooting of scenes that are slightly less critical to a film than those overseen by the main director.

set—The physical area where a movie is shot.

treatment—An artistic version or interpretation.

Universal Studios—One of the oldest and largest motion-picture studios in the world, founded in 1912 and located in Universal City, California.

BIBLIOGRAPHY

Barnes, Brooks. "Middle Earth Wizard's Not-So-Silent Partner." *New York Times* online edition, November 30, 2012. Retrieved January 16, 2014 from www.nytimes.com/2012/12/02/movies/middle-earth-wizards-not-so-silent-partner.html?pagewanted=2&_r=0

Berardinelli, James. "*Meet the Feebles*." Reelviews.net Movie Reviews, retrieved January 10, 2014 from www.reelviews.net/php_review_template.php?identifier=390

Jackson, Peter. "Sir Peter Jackson: Lord of the Cinema." Academy of Achievement online interview conducted June 3, 2006. Lumet, Sidney. *Making Movies*. New York, NY: Random House, 2010.

"Peter Jackson biography." Bio.com. Retrieved January 16, 2014 from www.biography.com/people/Peter-jackson-37009

Pryor, Ian. *Peter Jackson: From Prince of Splatter to Lord of the Rings, An Unauthorized Biography*. New York, NY: St. Martin's Press, 2003.

Ressner, Jeffrey. "Fantastic Voyage," *DGA Quarterly*, Summer 2013.

Ressner, Jeffery. "Fantastic Voyage." DGA.org, Summer 2013. Retrieved January 16, 2014 from www.dga.org/Craft/DGAQ/All-Articles/1303-Summer-2013/DGA-Interview-Peter-Jackson.aspx

Sibley, Brian. *Peter Jackson: A Filmmaker's Journey.* London, England: HarperCollins Entertainment, 2006.

Simpson, Paul. *Middle-Earth Envisioned: The Hobbit and the Lord of the Rings. On Screen, On Stage, and Beyond.* New York, NY: Race Point Publishing, 2013.

(Staff). "Exclusive Interview: Andy Serkis," *Total Film, The Modern Guide to Movies,* December 5, 2005.

Susman, Gary. "25 Things you didn't know about 'Lord of the Rings: The Fellowship of the Ring'" posted Dec. 19, 2011 on the Moviefone Blog, retrieved Dec. 30, 2013, at news.moviefone.com/2011/12/19/25-things-you-didnt-know-about-the-lord-of-the-rings-the-fellowship-of-the-ring/

Vary, Adam. "Why Guillermo del Toro Left *The Hobbit*—and Peter Jackson Will Not Replace Him as Director," *Entertainment Weekly,* May 31, 2010.

Whitaker, Sheila. "Saul Zaentz obituary: Oscar-winning film producer behind *One Flew Over the Cuckoo's Nest, Amadeus* and *The English Patient." The Guardian Online,* January 5, 2014. Retrieved January 16, 2014 from www.theguardian.com/film/2014/jan/05/saul-zaentz

Woods, Paul A. *Peter Jackson: From Gore to Mordor.* Medford, NJ: Plexus Publishing, 2005.

Woods, Sean. "Peter Jackson: Master of Middle Earth." RollingStone.com, February 19, 2013.

SOURCE NOTES

Chapter 1

Pg. 9: Peter Jackson, "Sir Peter Jackson: Lord of the Cinema." Academy of Achievement online interview conducted June 3, 2006. Retrieved January 9, 2014 from www.achievement.org/autodoc/page/jac0int-1

Pgs. 10–11: Jackson in Academy of Achievement online interview

Pgs. 14–15: Jackson in Academy of Achievement online interview

Chapter 2

Pg. 21: Jackson in Academy of Achievement online interview

Pgs. 25–26: James Berardinelli, "*Meet the Feebles.*" Reelviews Movie Reviews, retrieved January 10, 2014 from www.reelviews.net/php_review_template.php?identifier=390

Pg. 26: Jackson quoted by Sean Woods, "Peter Jackson: Master of Middle Earth." RollingStone.com, February 19, 2013. Retrieved January 13, 2014 from www.rollingstone.com/movies/news/q-a-Peter-jackson-master-of-middle-earth-20130219

Chapter 3

Pgs. 42–43: Howard Shore quoted by Gary Susman, "25 Things you didn't know about 'Lord of the Rings: The Fellowship of the Ring.'" Moviefone Blog, December 19, 2011. Retrieved January 28, 2014 from news.moviefone.com/2011/12/19/25-things-you-didnt-know-about-the-lord-of-the-rings-the-fellowship-of-the-ring/

Chapter 4

Pg. 51: Andy Serkis quoted by Total Film, "Exclusive Interview: Andy Serkis." TotalFilm.com, December 9, 2005. Retrieved January 28, 2014 from www.totalfilm.com/features/exclusive-interview-andy-serkis

Pg. 52: Jackson quoted by Total Film, "Final Day of Kong Week: Exclusive Interview with Peter Jackson" TotalFilm.com, December 15, 2005. Retrieved January 28, 2014 from www.totalfilm.com/features/final-day-of-kong-week-exclusive-interview-with-peter-jackson

Chapter 5

Pg. 67: Jackson quoted by Jeffrey Ressner, "Fantastic Voyage." DGA.org, Summer 2013. Retrieved January 28, 2014 from www.dga.org/Craft/DGAQ/All-Articles/1303-Summer-2013/DGA-Interview-Peter-Jackson.aspx

FURTHER INFORMATION

Books

Garza, Sarah. *Action! Making Movies*. Huntington Beach, CA: Teacher Created Materials, 2013.

Pryor, Ian. *Peter Jackson: From Prince of Splatter to Lord of the Rings*. New York, NY: Thomas Dunne, 2004.

Tolkien, J. R. R. *The Hobbit* (Illustrated Edition). New York, NY: Houghton Mifflin Harcourt, 2013.

Tolkien, J. R. R. *The Lord of the Rings* Trilogy (50th Anniversary Edition). New York, NY: Houghton Mifflin Harcourt, 2012.

Woods, Paul A. *Peter Jackson: From Gore to Mordor*. Medford, NJ: Plexus Publishing, 2005.

On the Web
Peter Jackson's Facebook page
www.facebook.com/PeterJacksonNZ

Peter Jackson's Facebook page is updated with lots of interesting things, including movie clips and production videos.

Internet Movie Database (IMDb.com) Peter Jackson page
www.imdb.com/name/nm0001392/

Information regarding Peter Jackson on the most comprehensive movie-industry data site on the Web. Loads of photos, videos, and links to other Jackson-related pages.

Box Office Mojo/Peter Jackson information
www.boxofficemojo.com/people/chart/?id=peterjackson.htm

All the information you'll ever need about the sales figures of Peter Jackson's films, as well as which studio distributed them, release dates, and so on.

INDEX

Page numbers in **boldface** are illustrations.

ABOUT THE AUTHOR

Wil Mara is a bestselling and award-winning author of more than 150 books, many of which are educational titles for children. For more information about his work, please visit www.wilmara.com.